Contents

How Small Is Small?

Is an ant big or small? Compared with a dust mite, it's enormous. However, a dust mite is absolutely huge compared with a tiny bacterium. What's more, a bacterium can be more than 20 times bigger than a virus.

There is a whole world that is too small for us to see without a microscope. There are millions of different kinds of **microbes** of all shapes and sizes. They feed and reproduce in different ways, and they live in almost every place on Earth.

There are so many different kinds of microbes that scientists have identified only a small percentage. However, they are able to place most newly discovered microbes into groups of similar microbes. This helps them understand what they have found.

This creepy creature is a dust mite. Thousands of them can live in a single ball of dust. They feed on the dead skin that we shed. Although we can barely spot them without a microscope, they are still too big to be considered true microbes.

Sizing Up Microbes

Not all bacteria are the same size. Neither are all viruses. However, this chart gives you an idea of the rough size of some small things compared with other small things.

Ant: $\frac{1}{8}$ inch

Dust mite: $\frac{1}{50}$ inch – more than six times smaller than an ant.

Bacterium: $\frac{1}{25{,}400}$ inch – more than 500 times smaller than a dust mite, and more than 3,000 times smaller than an ant.

Virus: $\frac{1}{508{,}000}$ inch – 20 times smaller than a bacterium, more than 10,000 times smaller than a dust mite, and 60,000 times smaller than an ant.

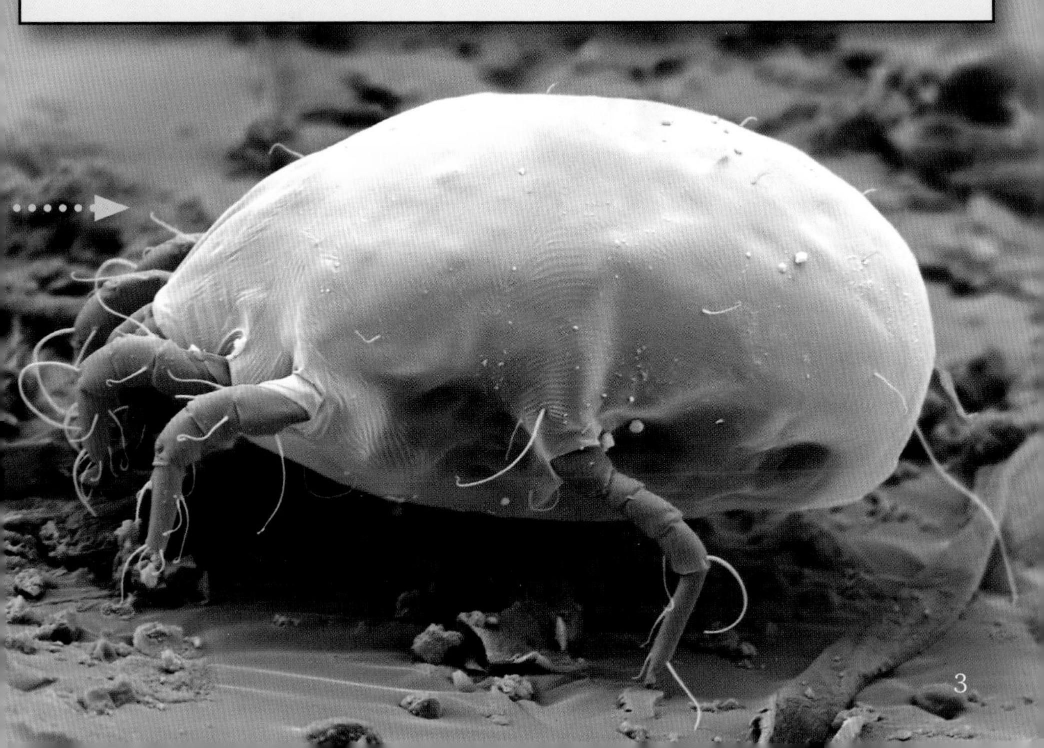

Mighty Microscopes

Without microscopes, we would know almost nothing about microbes. Microscopes are a **microbiologist**'s most important tool. Different kinds of microscopes magnify things by different amounts.

Ordinary light microscopes use glass lenses and light to magnify an object. They can magnify things by about 1,000 times. Light microscopes are very useful to microbiologists because they can be used to study living microbes. Scientists can watch microbes move, grow, and reproduce in front of their eyes.

However, light microscopes can't be used to see very small microbes, such as viruses. Scientists saw viruses for the first time in the 1930s, when the **electron** microscope was invented. Electron microscopes use a beam of electrons, rather than light, to magnify an image. Because electrons are very small – much smaller than a whole **atom** – they can **resolve** very small details. Some electron microscopes can magnify a specimen up to a million times.

This scientist is showing students an image of a tiny creature under a scanning electron microscope. The main part of the microscope is behind the boy. It doesn't have an eyepiece. Instead, it sends the image to a display screen.

The microscopes used in most schools are light microscopes. The sample is placed on a glass slide. The person looks through an eyepiece and then adjusts the knobs to bring the image into focus.

The Basics About Bacteria

You might have heard people mention bacteria when they were talking about germs. This is because many bacteria can cause diseases in other living things. However, describing all bacteria as germs is like describing all animals as meat-eaters. It's not true of the whole group.

Bacteria are one-celled microbes that are generally smaller and simpler than the cells that make up our bodies. There are millions of different kinds. Some are round, some are rod-shaped, and some are spiral-shaped. Some bacteria are like plants. They make their food using the energy in sunlight. Others feed on the food around them. They usually live in the places where they feed. This might be inside a person's body, inside a boiling mud pool, in a piece of rotting meat, or in soil.

Scientists call a round bacterium a *coccus*, a rod-shaped bacterium a *bacillus*, and a spiral-shaped bacterium a *spirillum*.

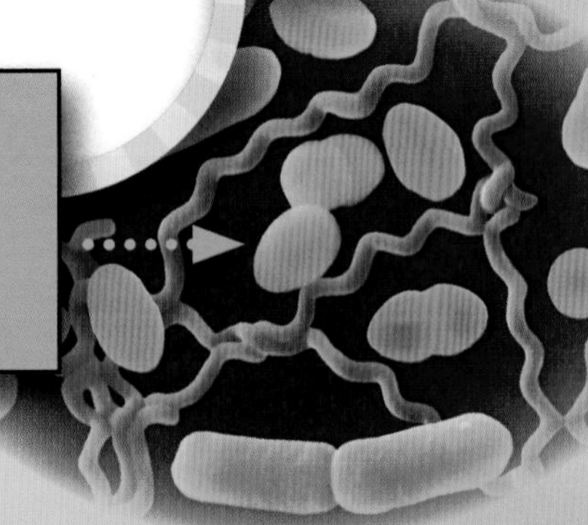

This electron microscope image shows bacteria on the tip of a pin.

Sometimes two or more bacteria link together. Chains of round bacteria are called *streptococci*. The bacterium *Streptococcus pyogenes* (below) causes sore throats and other health problems.

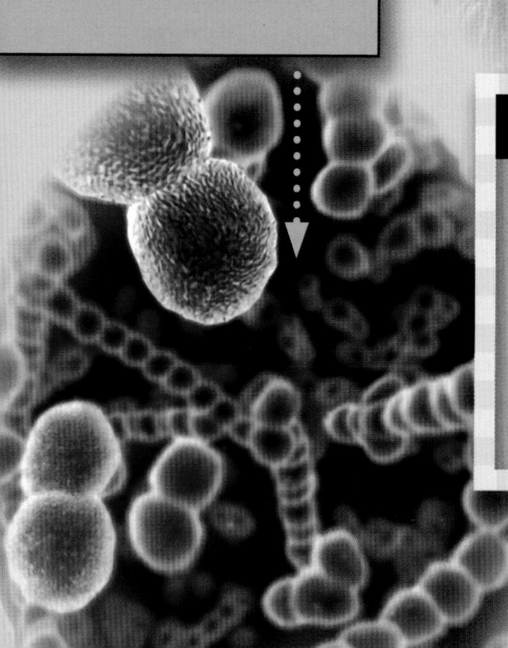

Mini Fact

Have you ever felt a fuzzy layer on your teeth? This is a layer of bacteria and food called plaque. Plaque bacteria produce an acid that causes tooth decay. Brushing your teeth removes the bacteria and the acid.

Plain Facts About Protists

Another big group of microbes is called protists. This group is even more varied than bacteria. The thing that most protists have in common is that they are made up of one quite complicated cell, which contains a **nucleus** like a plant or an animal cell. Most protists live in water or damp soil, but some live inside other living things. Some protists are animal-like, some are funguslike, and some are plantlike. However, these groups often overlap.

Animal-like protists are called protozoa (*pro tuh ZOH uh*). They surround food particles, taking them into their bodies. Some scientists group protozoans according to the way they move. They divide them into four main groups. They are:

- Protozoa that swim by waving a long tail called a flagellum (*fluh JEL um*)
- Protozoa that swim by waving many tiny hairlike structures called cilia (*SIH lee uh*)
- Protozoa that move or feed by changing shape
- Protozoa that glide. These protozoa are usually **parasites** that infect plants or animals.

These two protozoa live in pond water. They both move by waving their hairlike cilia. In this case, one is attacking the other, getting ready to consume it.

This amazing shell is the skeleton of a radiolarian. When it was alive, it fed by pushing out parts of its body into fingerlike shapes. The shapes went through the holes in the skeleton to trap food particles in the ocean.

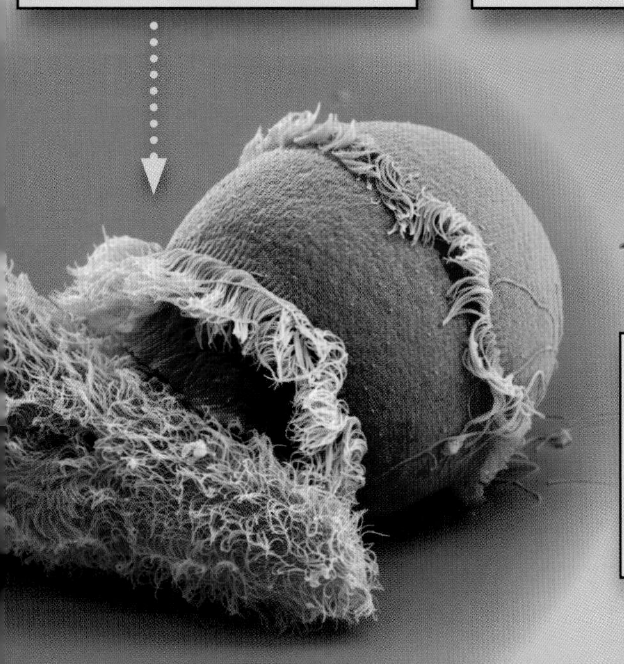

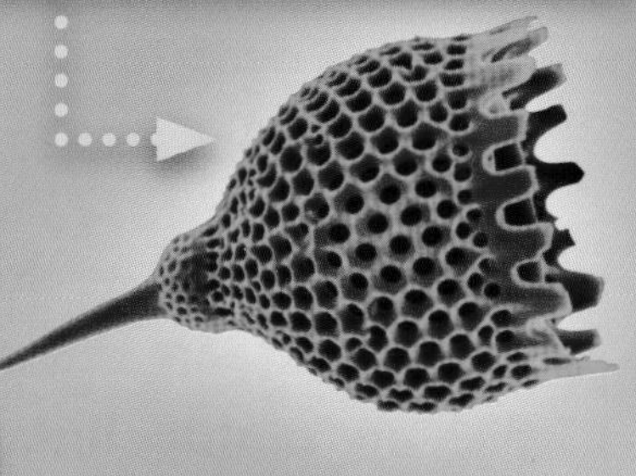

This submarine-shaped protozoan has a flagellum. It moves through water by waving the flagellum.

A protozoan causes the disease malaria. It is a parasite. When it infects a human red blood cell, it multiplies. Then many new malaria protozoa burst out of the cell.

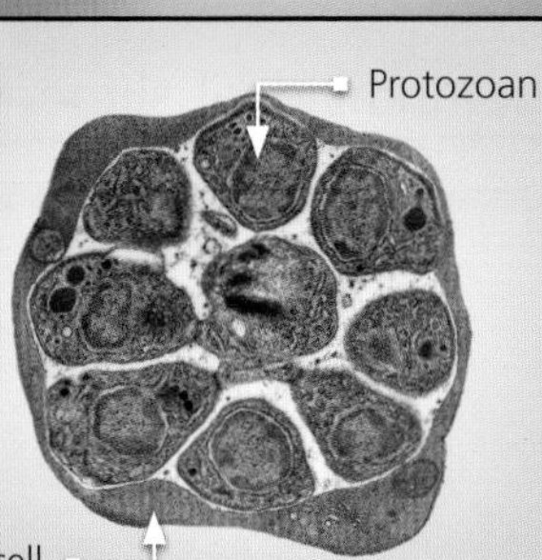

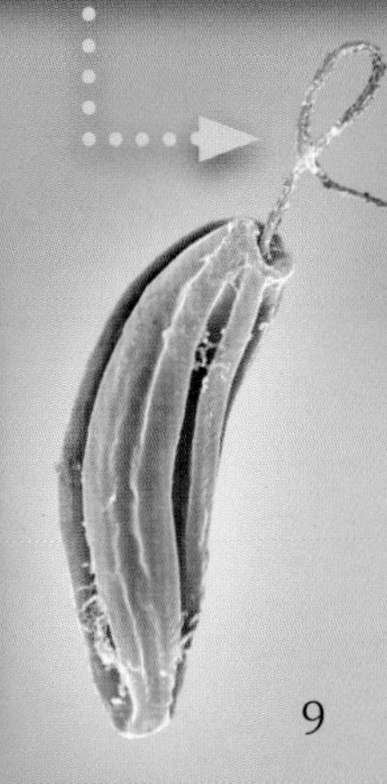

Plantlike protists have one big thing in common with plants. They contain a green substance called chlorophyll (*KLOR uh fil*), which they use to make their own food. Chlorophyll captures energy from sunlight to convert water and carbon dioxide into oxygen and sugars. The sugars provide food for the protist. Protists that make their own food don't need to move around to feed, and many of them are not able to move.

One-celled **algae** are sometimes considered to be plantlike protists. They are one-celled relatives of seaweeds, which are **multicellular** algae.

Slime molds are funguslike protists. Much of the time, they are single-celled organisms that live in the soil, feeding on bacteria and dead plant and animal matter. However, when food becomes scarce, hundreds of them sometimes join together to form a sluglike shape. This moves around for a while and then stops and produces **spores**. The spores are blown by the wind to new places where they grow into new, individual slime molds.

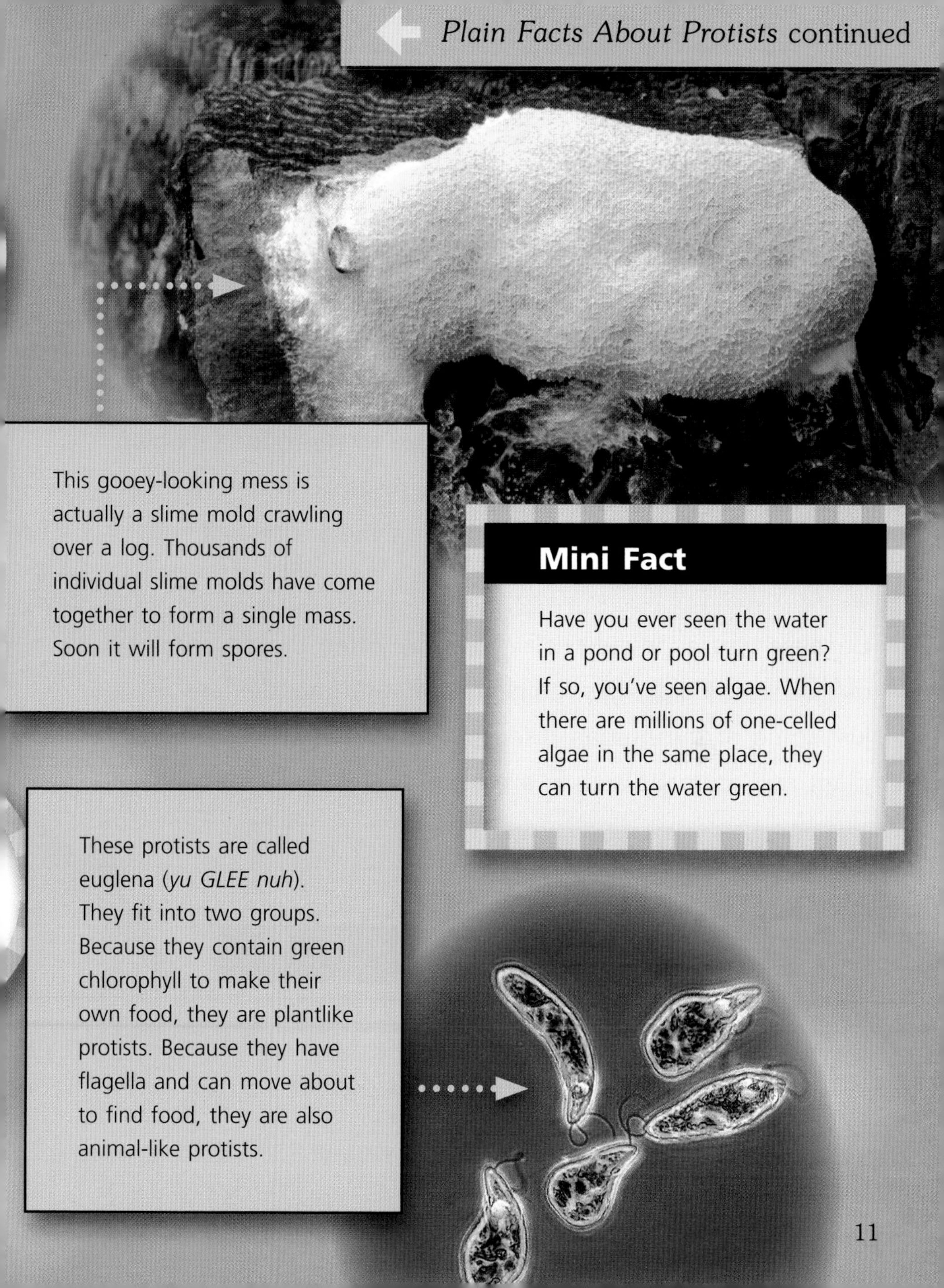

This gooey-looking mess is actually a slime mold crawling over a log. Thousands of individual slime molds have come together to form a single mass. Soon it will form spores.

Mini Fact

Have you ever seen the water in a pond or pool turn green? If so, you've seen algae. When there are millions of one-celled algae in the same place, they can turn the water green.

These protists are called euglena (*yu GLEE nuh*). They fit into two groups. Because they contain green chlorophyll to make their own food, they are plantlike protists. Because they have flagella and can move about to find food, they are also animal-like protists.

Vile Facts About Viruses

A virus is different from other living things in one very important way. It does not have a cell structure. It is smaller than a cell, and it doesn't contain all the things needed for life. For example, a virus cannot reproduce on its own. To reproduce, a virus invades a plant, animal, or bacterial cell. Then it uses that cell's chemistry to reproduce its own **genetic material** and make new viruses. The new viruses burst out of the cell, often killing it in the process. They then go on to infect other cells.

Because viruses invade cells, they are often the cause of diseases. Colds, flus, chicken pox, and measles are just some of the human diseases caused by viruses. Many plant and animal diseases are also caused by viruses.

Mini Fact

Have you ever had the flu? If so, you've had a **viral** infection. However, it wasn't the viruses that made your nose run or made you sneeze. Your body did that to clear the viruses out of your nose and throat.

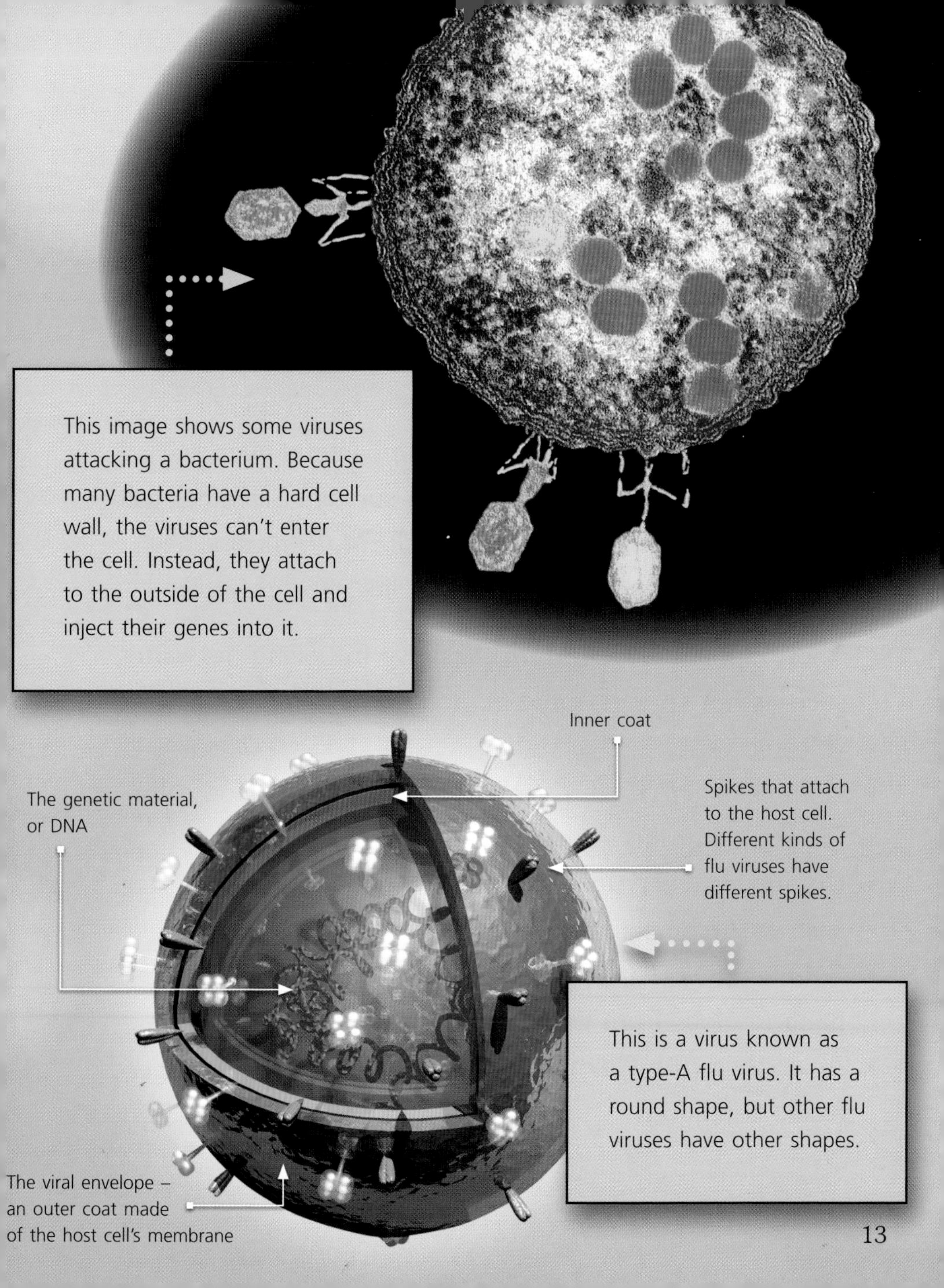
This image shows some viruses attacking a bacterium. Because many bacteria have a hard cell wall, the viruses can't enter the cell. Instead, they attach to the outside of the cell and inject their genes into it.
Inner coat
The genetic material, or DNA
Spikes that attach to the host cell. Different kinds of flu viruses have different spikes.
This is a virus known as a type-A flu virus. It has a round shape, but other flu viruses have other shapes.
The viral envelope – an outer coat made of the host cell's membrane

Microbes to the Max

Microbes are important in all **ecosystems**. Many of them are **decomposers**. Without them, the nutrients in dead plants and animals would not be returned to the soil, and the cycle of life would grind to a halt.

Most microbes cause us no harm. They are in the air, in water, and on most surfaces. Some bacteria even live in places where no other life forms can survive. Scientists call these microbes extremophiles (*ex TREEM uh files*). They group them according to where they live. For example:

- Thermophiles (*THURM uh files*) live in boiling hot water, such as hot springs, geysers, and underwater volcanic vents.
- Halophiles (*HAY luh files*) live in water that is too salty for any other life forms, such as the Dead Sea.
- Cryophiles (*CRY uh files*) live in very cold places, such as Arctic soil, ice, snow, and glaciers.
- Snotites (*SNOT ites*) are colonies of bacteria that hang in globs from the roofs of caves.
- Acidophiles (*uh CID uh files*) live in very acidic conditions.

The microbes in a compost heap soon break down food scraps into compost. The compost is rich in nutrients that will help other plants grow.

Thermophiles help produce some of the amazing colors in this hot spring in Yellowstone National Park.

The Dead Sea is so salty that people can float in it very easily. It is too salty for fish to live in. However, it is full of halophiles. These bacteria can live only in very salty water. If they were put in ordinary sea water, they would die.

Microbes and Food

Before people even knew that microbes existed, they were using them to create foods. Dairy products such as cheese, sour cream, and yogurt are made by letting specific bacteria turn milk sour. For thousands of years, people have used yeasts to make bread rise. A yeast is a one-celled fungus. It feeds on sugars in the bread dough and gives off bubbles of carbon dioxide gas, which make the dough rise.

We use some microbes to prevent the growth of other microbes. Vinegar, for example, is made by adding yeast to fruit juice, grains, or sugar to make alcohol. Then a particular bacterium turns the alcohol into vinegar. Vinegar is so acidic that it kills many microbes. This means that we can store food in vinegar to keep it from going bad.

When unwanted microbes get into human food, they can cause problems. We become aware of their presence when food goes moldy or slimy, or if it smells rotten. Rotten food must be thrown away because some microbes produce poisons that can make people very ill.

Cucumbers are often pickled in salt and vinegar. In the days before refrigerators, pickling was one way people preserved fruits and vegetables for winter.

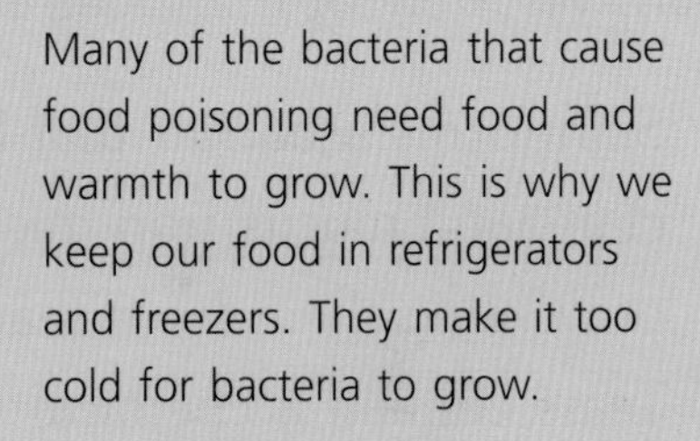

Many of the bacteria that cause food poisoning need food and warmth to grow. This is why we keep our food in refrigerators and freezers. They make it too cold for bacteria to grow.

When a yeast cell reproduces, it forms a bud that grows into a new yeast cell. This yeast cell has scars that show the places where buds have formed and broken off.

Mini Fact

Have you ever seen a label on milk or cheese saying *pasteurized*? This means that the food has been heated to a very high temperature to kill off any harmful microbes.

Microbes and Health

Many bacteria live in our intestines. They have an important job to do. They use up all the space and nutrients available so that harmful microbes cannot establish themselves. Some bacteria also have other jobs, such as helping with digestion and producing vitamins K and B.

The microbes on our skin also crowd out harmful bacteria. Although there are millions of microbes in the air and on our skin, very few of them get inside our bodies. This is because:

- Skin forms a barrier that keeps out microbes.
- Hairs and mucus trap microbes that get into the nose, preventing them from reaching the lungs.
- Tears contain a chemical that kills microbes that get into the eyes.
- The stomach acid that breaks down food also kills many microbes that get swallowed.

In spite of these defenses, some microbes still manage to infect us. This is when the immune system gets involved. The immune system has special cells that track down and destroy microbes in the blood or body tissues.

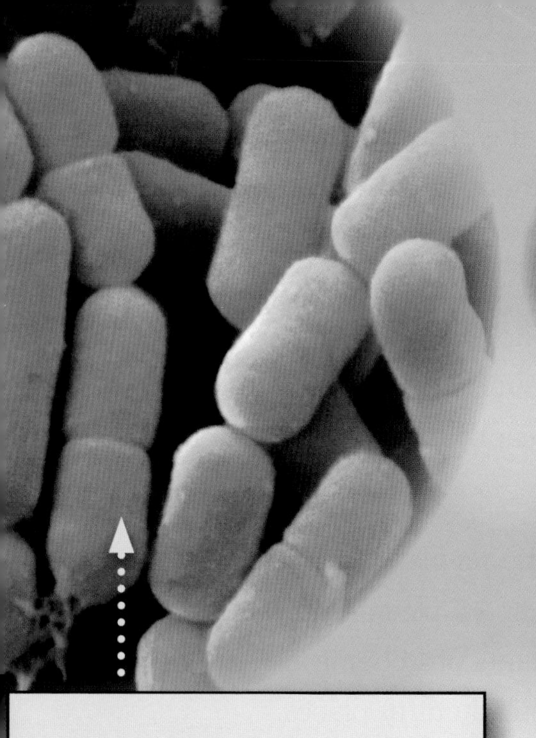

These rod-shaped bacteria live inside human intestines. They help the body get rid of harmful bacteria that can cause diseases.

As we get older, our bodies produce more sweat. Warm, sweaty places, such as the armpits and between the toes, make homes for the kinds of microbes that release smelly chemicals. A daily shower, however, will wash most of them away.

Vaccinations can help the body to fight harmful microbes. An injection of dead or weakened microbes allows the immune system to recognize that microbe and build up its defenses. This means that it can fight that microbe if it encounters it again.

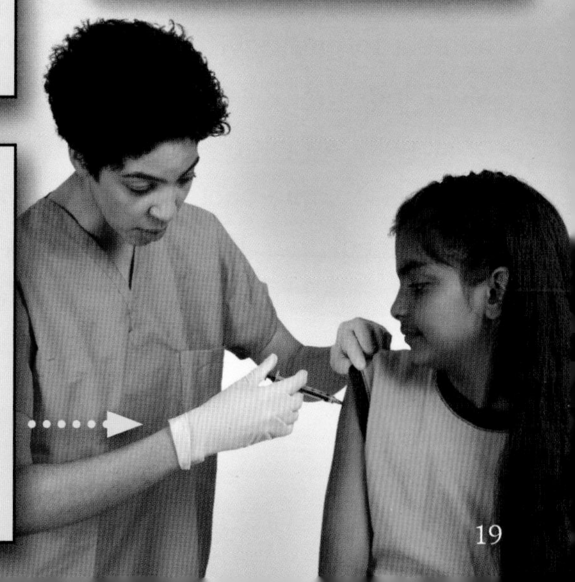

Microbes are part of the natural world. It is not good for your health or the environment to try to kill off all the microbes around you. However, there are some easy ways you can help get rid of harmful microbes. The simplest way is to wash regularly. A mild soap and warm water is all you need to remove most harmful microbes from your skin. If a cut becomes infected, antiseptic creams can help kill the invading microbes.

It is also helpful to keep your home clean, especially the kitchen and bathroom. Ordinary cleaning products remove many germs. Disinfectants are chemicals that help kill the microbes in particularly dirty places.

Sometimes a microbe gets through the body's defense system and makes a person ill. In these cases, a doctor may be able to give advice or prescribe medicines that will help. Medicines that kill bacteria are called antibiotics. If you are prescribed antibiotics, it important to finish the course. Otherwise some bacteria may survive and become **resistant** to the medicine. This is a problem because some diseases are becoming harder to cure with antibiotics.

When you sneeze, thousands of microbes are propelled into the air. This is why you should sneeze into tissues, especially when you are unwell. Harmful microbes can also be spread to the surfaces that sick people touch, so it is important to wash your hands regularly.

Mini Fact

Have you ever had a cold or flu and been told by your doctor that antibiotics won't help? This is because colds and flus are viral infections, and antibiotics kill bacteria, not viruses.

Sometimes antibiotic medicines kill off the healthful bacteria in our bodies as well as the unhealthful ones. It is thought that eating yogurt after a course of antibiotics can help. Live yogurt contains living bacteria of the kind needed by our intestines.

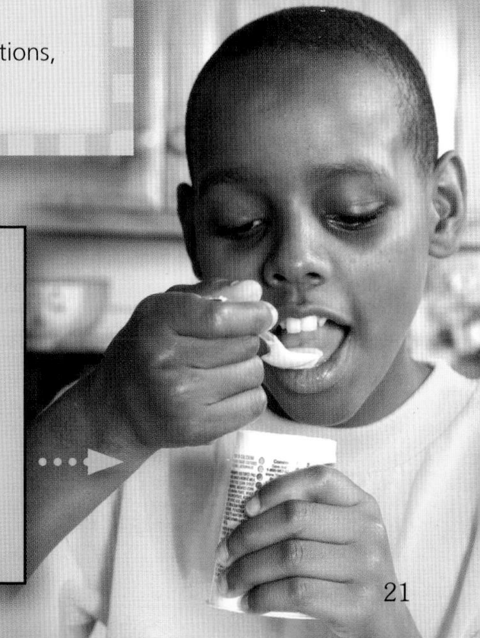

Microbes and the Future

Some microbiologists work in laboratories. They use microbes in experiments. For example, many microbiologists are looking for cures for diseases. They keep samples of bacteria frozen in very cold freezers. The freezers don't kill the bacteria, they just keep them **dormant**, where they don't move or grow. Then, when the scientists need to use the bacteria, they thaw them out and place them in flasks containing warm water and nutrients. Within hours, a small **colony** of bacteria will start reproducing. Soon there will be millions in the flask.

Scientists are discovering many new ways that people can use microbes. For example, people already use bacteria to clean up oil spills. Extra nutrients are sometimes added to the oil spill to allow oil-eating bacteria to reproduce quickly. When the oil is gone, the bacteria population dies back. Until recently, this has been possible only in warm places. Now scientists are finding extremophiles in cold places, such as Antarctica, that can do the same job.

Sometimes microbiologists grow bacteria on dishes of a special jelly. Although one bacterium is too small to see, a colony of thousands forms an easy-to-see blob on the jelly.

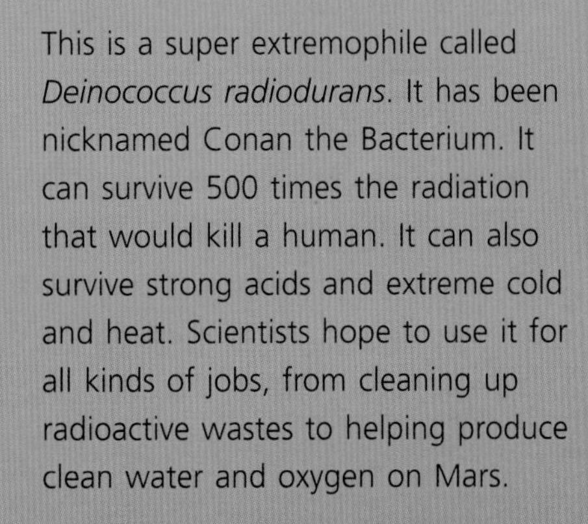

This is a super extremophile called *Deinococcus radiodurans*. It has been nicknamed Conan the Bacterium. It can survive 500 times the radiation that would kill a human. It can also survive strong acids and extreme cold and heat. Scientists hope to use it for all kinds of jobs, from cleaning up radioactive wastes to helping produce clean water and oxygen on Mars.

This microbiologist is inspecting a flask in which she is growing a colony of bacteria. The nutrients have made the liquid yellow. It will get thicker as the bacteria reproduce.

Glossary

algae a group of rootless plants and plantlike living things that live in water or damp places. It includes seaweeds and some one-celled protists.

atom the tiniest part of an element that has the properties of that element

colony a group of living things of the same kind living in the same place

decomposer a living thing that feeds on the remains of other living things

dormant in an inactive state; alive but not moving, growing, or feeding

ecosystem the plants, animals, and non-living things that share a place and affect one another

electron a tiny particle that moves around the center of an atom

genetic material the genes, or DNA, inside a cell, which contain information about the characteristics of that living thing

microbe a tiny living thing that can be seen only with a microscope

microbiologist a scientist who studies microbes

multicellular made up of many cells

nucleus a particular part of a cell that contains the genetic material

parasite a living thing that lives and feeds in or on another living thing

resistant not affected by something, or able to oppose its effects

resolve to make something clear and easy to see

spore a seedlike structure that grows into a new living thing

viral to do with a virus

Index